BUBBA WALLACE

KENNY ABDO

Fly!

An Imprint of Abdo Zoom

abdobooks.com

abdobooks.com

Published by Abdo Zoom, a division of ABDO, P.O. Box 398166, Minneapolis,
Minnesota 55439. Copyright © 2022 by Abdo Consulting Group, Inc. International
copyrights reserved in all countries. No part of this book may be reproduced in any
form without written permission from the publisher. Fly!™ is a trademark and logo
of Abdo Zoom.

Printed in the United States of America, North Mankato, Minnesota.
102021
012022

Photo Credits: Getty Images, iStock, Shutterstock, U.S. Air Force, ©Nascarking p.15 /
CC BY-SA 4.0
Production Contributors: Kenny Abdo, Jennie Forsberg, Grace Hansen
Design Contributors: Candice Keimig, Neil Klinepier

Library of Congress Control Number: 2021940199

Publisher's Cataloging-in-Publication Data

Names: Abdo, Kenny, author.
Title: Bubba Wallace / by Kenny Abdo
Description: Minneapolis, Minnesota : Abdo Zoom, 2022 | Series: NASCAR
    biographies | Includes online resources and index.
Identifiers: ISBN 9781098226787 (lib. bdg.) | ISBN 9781644946817 (pbk.) |
    ISBN 9781098227623 (ebook) | ISBN 9781098228040 (Read-to-Me ebook)
Subjects: LCSH: Wallace, Bubba, 1993---Juvenile literature. | Automobile racing
    drivers--Biography--Juvenile literature. | Stock car drivers--Biography--Juvenile
    literature. | NASCAR (Association)--Juvenile literature. | African American
    athletes--Biography--Juvenile literature. | Stock car racing--Juvenile literature.
Classification: DDC 796.72092--dc23

TABLE OF CONTENTS

BUBBA WALLACE

Making history and tire marks,
Bubba Wallace has changed
the face of NASCAR in his
short career.

As one of the only Black NASCAR drivers, Wallace focused on both winning and **advocating** for more **diversity** in the sport.

EARLY YEARS

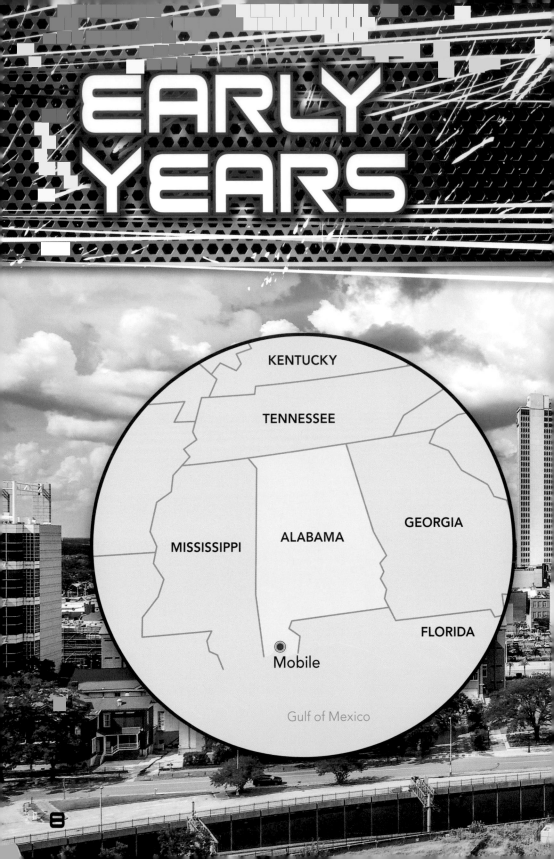

KENTUCKY

TENNESSEE

GEORGIA

MISSISSIPPI

ALABAMA

FLORIDA

⊙ Mobile

Gulf of Mexico

Darrell Wallace Jr. was born in Mobile, Alabama, in 1993. His sister nicknamed him 'Bubba' the day he was born.

Bubba's family moved to Concord, North Carolina, when he was just two years old. It was there that he quickly caught the racing bug. By age nine, Bubba had already learned to drive.

At 17, Bubba won his first race in the K&N Pro Series East. He raced one more season on the **circuit** before moving up to a NASCAR **series**.

THE BIG TIME

In 2013, Wallace had the fastest lap in qualifying for the Lucas Oil 200. He became the youngest **pole** winner in the history of that truck **series**.

That same year, Wallace won the Kroger 200. He was the second Black driver to win a NASCAR national touring **series** race after Wendell Scott had in 1963.

In 2015, Wallace moved up to the NASCAR Xfinity Series. He drove the No. 6 Ford until the 2017 season.

Wallace drove the Nickelodeon Green Slime Ford in the 2017 NASCAR XFINITY Series. He finished with a top 10. Wallace went on to finish in second place at the 2018 **Daytona 500**.

NBA star Michael Jordan started the 23XI Racing NASCAR team in 2020. Wallace was chosen to be the team's main driver in 2021.

Wallace has been both in movies and on TV. He leant his voice to the 2017 movie *Cars 3*. In 2018, Facebook released a reality show *Behind the Wall: Bubba Wallace*.

Wallace founded and runs the Live to be Different Foundation. The **charity** supports people who need educational, medical, and social help.

Bubba Wallace journeyed through the racing world to become the only **full-time** Black driver in NASCAR and one of the most compelling athletes in the sport's history!

GLOSSARY

advocate – to publicly support a cause or policy.

charity – an organization set up to provide help and raise money for those in need.

circuit – another name for a track that races are held on.

Daytona 500 – the most famous stock car race in the world and one of the races in the Sprint Cup Series.

diversity – the practice or quality of including people from a range of different backgrounds.

full-time – working the full amount of someone's available time professionally.

pole – the fastest time in qualifying.

series – a racing season that consists of several races.

ONLINE RESOURCES

Booklinks
NONFICTION NETWORK
FREE! ONLINE NONFICTION RESOURCES

To learn more about Bubba Wallace, please visit **abdobooklinks.com** or scan this QR code. These links are routinely monitored and updated to provide the most current information available.

INDEX